SO-BFL-309

YOUR ECONOMIC LIFE
The Practical Applications of Economics

A Student Guide to Accompany
Economics Today
1999-2000 Edition

Roger LeRoy Miller
Institute for University Studies
Arlington, Texas

ADDISON-WESLEY

An imprint of Addison Wesley Longman, Inc.

Reading, Massachusetts • Menlo Park, California • New York • Harlow, England
Don Mills, Ontario • Sydney • Mexico City • Madrid • Amsterdam

Your Economic Life to accompany Miller, *Economics Today, 1999-2000 Edition*

Copyright © 1999 Addison Wesley Longman, Inc.

All rights reserved. Printed in the United States of America. No part of these materials may be used or reproduce in any manner whatsoever without written permission from the publisher, except testing materials, transparencie and transparency masters may be copied for classroom use. For information, address Addison Wesley Education Publishers Inc., One Jacob Way, Reading, Massachusetts 01867-3999.

ISBN:0-321-03363-9

3 4 5 6 7 8 9 10-CRS-02010099

PRELIMINARY STUDY TIPS

Fear can best describe the feelings of many beginning economics students prior to taking the course. Economics has often been labeled a "hard" subject to master. But it need not be. Here is a two-page plan of study for all chapters that allows you to learn the course material, enables you to apply economics to the world around you, and dispels the myth that economics is a more difficult topic to understand than others.

How to Learn Economics Using *Economics Today*

1) Read the *Preview Questions*. Can you think of answers to them? Do you have any preconceived notions about the topic to be discussed in each chapter?

2) Read the assigned chapter relatively rapidly without attempting to understand portions of it that you find difficult. Put it away for a few hours or even a day.

3) Reread the chapter, stopping at each point where you have difficulty and noting such difficulties on a separate sheet of paper. Look at the *Concepts in Brief* when you first encounter them. Do they make sense? If they don't, it means you missed an important theoretical concept or its application. Go back and reread the appropriate sections.

4) Draw the graphs yourself, reading their legends in the book as you do so. Do they make sense? How do they apply to the chapter materials?

5) Read each assigned *Issue and Application*, first looking at the *Concepts Applied*. Do the concepts mean anything to you? If they do, try to see where they fit into the analysis in the materials that follow. Try to answer the *For Critical Analysis* questions that appear at the end of each issue and application. How do the questions relate to the *Concepts Applied* that started the *Issues and Applications*? In most cases, you should be able to see a link.

6) Read through the glossary items in the margins. By now they should all be familiar.

7) Read the point-by-point *Chapter Summary*. Do all the points make sense? If not, review the appropriate sections.

8) Go back to the *Preview Questions* at the beginning of the chapter. Try to write down some ideas on you answers. Now refer to the answers given at the end of the chapter after the *Chapter Summary*.

9) Work through the odd-numbered *Problems* (and the even-numbered ones if they are assigned as homework). Do not look at the answers in the back of the book until you have worked the problem through. It is essentially a self-test system that shows you whether you have mastered one or more of the theoretical points in the chapter.

10) Use the separate *Study Guide*. This may be particularly appropriate just prior to examinations. If you have mastered the chapter materials, the *Study Guide* will reinforce your mastery of them and also improve your ability to do well on exams. You may wish to write your answers to the *Study Guide* questions on a separate piece of paper the first time you do them, then use the *Guide* as a refresher for the final examination, marking your answers one final time in the book and checking them with the correct answers. Also go to **www.econtoday.com** .

11) Additionally, in your preparation for midterm and final exams, you should reread the chapter once again, then go back and look at the *Preview Questions*, answering them with ease this time. Look at the *Concepts in Brief* highlighted throughout each chapter. Then go to the point-by-point *Chapter Summary*. All the concepts covered should be well understood by now.

12) After midterm examination, find out which questions you did not answer correctly. Go back to the *Study Guide*. Remember, use the midterm exams as a learning device rather than as a pure testing device.

13) Use the Web site for this text—**www.econ.com**—to study for your exams.

Introduction

Y ou may have heard somewhere that economics has been called the "dismal science." While it is true that a number of important concepts in economics are best understood from a theoretical perspective and are often most easily explained by using graphs, much of the usefulness of economic theory can be found in its application to your personal economic life. That is to say, lurking behind such concepts as opportunity cost, present value, supply and demand, and competitive markets are applications to your everyday life.

In this guide, I attempt to show some of those applications. In so doing my goal is to help you not only to retain the most important principles that you will learn by using *Economics Today*, 1999-2000 Edition, but also to allow you to apply them to problems that face you today, tomorrow, and for the rest of your life. Perhaps I am being presumptuous in believing that I can accomplish this task in a booklet this short. I'll let you be the judge.

On Doing Things Almost Well

P erhaps you have been told by well-meaning friends or relatives that you should strive for perfection. A common proverb is: "If something is worth doing, it is worth doing well." Now what exactly can that mean with respect to your life? Does it mean that every time you undertake *any* task you should continue doing that task until you are certain you have reached your version of perfection, or at least until you are certain you can do no better? I think not.

Every one of you is faced with constraints. Indeed, life is one big hassle with the constraints that face each one of us. A major constraint in your life is time. Everyone faces a scarcity of time. Therefore, while you are engaging in the job of doing something to perfection, you are not engaging in any other job (or any other pleasure for that matter). Otherwise stated, every action on your part involves an **opportunity cost**, defined in Chapter 2 of *Economics Today,* as the *value of the next-best alternative.* The quest for perfection involves use of time and hence is costly to you—you must give up other valuable alternatives to achieve it.

Let's consider an example. The words you are reading right now are words that I put down on paper. I had to spend time developing an outline for this guide, writing down a first draft, correcting that draft in order to write a second draft. Then I sent the manuscript to a large number of individuals—my colleagues—who wrote criticisms right on the manuscript. When I got back those comments, I had to go through them and decide which ones were valid for my purposes and which ones were not. I incorporated many of them in the third and final draft of the manuscript. Then I sent it to my publisher, Addison-Wesley, for type composition, printing, binding, and distribution. During the printing process I had to proof the resulting pages for any typographical errors.

Now why did I only do three drafts of this guide? Certainly I could have improved on what you are reading by sending the third draft out for review and then rewriting it. Also, I read the printed page proofs three times before I approved the result. I could have read them four times or five times. Whatever typographical errors are still in this booklet would probably have been caught. But I didn't write a fourth draft and I didn't read the printed page proofs again. Why not? Because I made a decision that the additional benefits from the additional work would not be worth the additional costs to me.

How did I calculate the benefits and how did I calculate the cost? With respect to the benefits, I looked at the potential improvement in the guide and how much more positively you and your professors would respond to an additional draft or an additional proofreading. I examined the additional cost, called the **marginal cost**, as the value of the time I would have had to give up to do that extra work. I didn't have an exact number in my head, but I knew I would take away time, for example, from extra research and proofreading for the 1999-2000 Edition of *Economics Today*.

So what you are reading is the result of an implicit comparison by me of the costs and benefits of my actions. I think this guide is well done, but I know it is not perfect. In *most* situations, whatever *you* do will not be perfect either because you must incur an opportunity cost to achieve perfection: the value of the time you use in any job.

Your rule of thumb should be as follows:

> **Undertake any activity up to the point at which the marginal benefit equals the marginal cost.**

This rule usually does not lead to perfection. It applies to studying for exams, polishing your car, looking for a video to rent, or working on a report that your boss wants next week. You'll find this same rule in many chapters in *Economics Today*. For example, the hiring decisions by any employer are made in this way.

Get All the Education You Can Get, or Maybe Not

When you are in junior high it starts. Your parents, relatives, and other adults start telling you that education is important, that it is *the* most important thing you'll ever do. They are probably right for most of us at that point in our lives. By the time you are in high school you are told by the same well-meaning adults that college is a great thing. And it is for most people. But then they sometimes tell you to "get all the education you can get." That's when well-meaning adults start misdirecting you.

If you were to take their advice seriously, you would plan a higher-education career consisting of a bachelor's degree, a master's degree, several Ph.D.s, and a number of post-doctoral fellowships. Then, indeed, you would be getting all the education you could get. Some people actually do that, but not very many. In fact, a relatively small percentage of adults go to graduate school and get an advanced degree. Despite what your parents may have told you, those people who don't get advanced degrees are more than likely behaving rationally.

What does rational mean in this instance? It means applying the rule of thumb given in the section above. One does not engage in any activity past the point at which marginal benefit equals marginal cost. Going to school year after year eventually leads to the point at which marginal cost exceeds marginal benefit.

What happens, of course, is that the **law of diminishing marginal returns** enters in to the learning process in which you are engaged. After a while, the incremental benefit of learning new skills starts decreasing as you continue to increase the inputs—your time, work effort, and money income. At some point this decreasing marginal benefit drops below the increasing marginal cost. Why does marginal cost increase? It increases because as you obtain more education and get older, your earning capacity goes up. That means that your opportunity cost of *not* working (your forgone income because you are still in school) thereby goes up.

My advice is, of course, stay in school—but only up to the point at which the marginal benefit of doing so just equals the marginal cost.

The Importance of Thinking Marginally

One concept that you have to get used to is that economists think about marginal changes. This has been the essence of much of the discussion so far. I have pointed to marginal benefits and marginal cost. **Marginal analysis** is the application of marginal thinking to a particular problem. Marginal thinking allows you to make choices that will maximize the value of any resource you have, including your time. One important result of using marginal analysis is that you do not waste your time worrying about what economists call sunk costs. **Sunk costs** are those that are not affected by the decision at hand. The only thing that matters are marginal costs—those costs that are affected by the decision at hand.

Consider one example: waiting in line to renew your driver's license. Does it matter how long you have waited in line? Not really, for that is a sunk cost. You cannot change the fact that you have already waited in line, say, one hour. The only thing that you can change is whether you wait in line any longer or leave, only to have to come back another day. Your decision to leave or to stay should be based on your prediction of how many more minutes it will take before you get your driver's license compared to the cost in time and effort of returning back to the driver licensing office and waiting in line again. If you knew for certain, for example, that at a particular time when you could come back you would only have to wait five minutes, and that if you continued to stand in line you would wait another half an hour, then you should leave. Your decision has nothing to do with the fact that you have waited in line one hour. That is a sunk cost.

Consider another example. You own a restaurant that is only open for dinner. You are trying to decide whether you should be open for lunch. If you ask your accountant, she may include as a cost of staying open at lunch some proportion of the rent, insurance, and other fixed costs. But these sunk costs are irrelevant. You pay them whether you stay open for lunch or not. The only thing that matters is a comparison of the marginal cost of staying open for lunch compared to the marginal benefit—which would be your increased *net* revenues.

The same analysis holds for an airline. If an accountant tells the airline manager that the "full" cost of transporting one passenger from Boston to Portland is $250, does that mean no passenger should be charged less then $250? The answer is probably, no. Much of the $250 cost calculated by the accountant must be paid whether the plane carries 50 passengers or 150 passengers. The cost of fuel, maintenance, depreciation, insurance, and labor is the same whether the plane is full or empty. What is the marginal cost of transporting one more passenger from Boston to Portland? It might be, say, $125. Therefore, if the airline can entice a senior citizen to fly from Boston to Portland for $200, the airline is better off—it will make higher profits overall. If it can entice a large number of individuals to go on stand-by in order to fly at the reduced rate, the airline will make even greater profits. The relevant costs for deciding whether to carry lower-priced passengers include only the extra cost of processing additional tickets, providing food and beverage, the additional fuel because of the extra weight, and so on. These are the relevant costs.

Paying Rent: Is it Throwing Good Money Away?

One of the American dreams is to own a house. For many Americans, this dream comes true. On a per-person basis, more Americans live in single-family dwellings than do citizens in any other country. There are lots of good reasons to want to own a house, not the least being pride of ownership. Other benefits of owning a house include the ability to customize it to your own tastes and thereby give you more of a feeling of being "at home." Also, any improvements in the structure or the land accrue to you, the owner, when you resell the house. And certainly we cannot forget that the purchase of a house and land has turned out to be a good and sometimes spectacular investment for many Americans. For example, those people who purchased houses many years ago in most parts of California received a very high rate of return for a while. That is to say, the values of their property went up much faster than the rate of inflation.

All of that sounds so good, one wonders why anyone would ever rent. After all, rent payments simply go to a land-lord, never to be seen again. Any increase in the market value of the house and land benefits the landlord, not the tenants. Hence, the common-sense notion is that paying rent is throwing away wealth.

Not so fast. A few important economic concepts have been lost in this simplified analysis. The most important is oppor-tunity cost, a concept that permeates almost all economic analy-sis, particularly that which applies to your personal economic decisions. When you purchase a house, you have a large num-ber of costs to consider. They are the following:

1. Maintenance and repairs due to the physical depre-ciation of the structure.
2. Insurance.
3. Electricity and heating fuel.
4. Mortgage payments.

The last item is the crucial one. Somehow, it seems better to make **mortgage payments**—payments on a loan taken out to purchase your own house—than it does to pay rent to a land-lord. After all, the popular notion goes, you are at least "investing" in your own property.

There is a cost to that investment, however. When you purchase a house you typically have to make a **down pay-ment**. Consider an example. You buy a $200,000 house and put 25 percent down. You have invested $50,000. Every year you incur an opportunity cost because of that $50,000 invest-ment, because you could, for example, put that $50,000 in a bank and earn interest. The interest you earn may be taxable by federal and state governments, but you are still left with a posi-tive after-tax return when you place that $50,000 in the bank.

Let's say that after any taxes owed, you can earn 5 percent by placing this $50,000 in the bank. Five percent of $50,000 equals $2,500. $2,500 is therefore the annual opportunity cost of that $50,000 down payment.

Here is a numerical example to consider. We'll assume that the opportunity cost of your down payment is $2,400 a year, or exactly $200 a month. Then let's add the other costs of owning a house expressed on a *monthly* basis:

Opportunity cost of down payment	$200
Insurance	$100
Repairs	$150
Miscellaneous	<u>$75</u>
TOTAL	<u>$525</u>

Let's say that you could rent equivalent housing at $450 a month. Should you rent? The answer depends on your prediction about the *appreciation* in the market value of the house. If you think that it will appreciate at more than $75 per month ($900 per year) then you should buy the house. If you think it will appreciate at less than $75 a month, you should probably rent.

Don't quickly jump to the conclusion that the market value of any house *has to* appreciate. Just because you may have observed housing prices going up in some cities doesn't necessarily mean that the market value of the house you choose to buy will go up every year. In some areas of the country, housing values have fallen, sometimes dramatically.

We Couldn't Afford to Buy This House if We Had to Buy it Today

There has been considerable appreciation in the market value of houses and land in various parts of the country. Families of modest means may find themselves living in houses that they paid, say, $70,000 for but could sell for $200,000 to even $500,000 today. A common reaction to such a situation is to say that "We couldn't live in this house if we had to buy it today." What these individuals are ignoring is that in fact *they are already paying* today to live in the house.

Consider two families that are living in identical houses with identical plots of land, but in different parts of the country. The market value of one family's house is $100,000 and the market value of the other family's house is $500,000. To make the example clear, further assume that neither family is making mortgage payments. Assume further that all costs of maintenance, repairs, real estate taxes, and electricity are exactly the same for both families. Even under these highly unrealistic assumptions, the family living in the $500,000 house is paying *five times* as much for housing *services* as the family living in the $100,000 house, even though the houses are physically identical! Each family has the option of selling its house and investing the funds and making a positive after-tax rate of return, say 5 percent per year. Five percent of $100,000 is $5,000 per year. Five percent of $500,000 is $25,000 per year. The family that owns the $500,000 house is therefore paying five times more in opportunity cost each year to live in its dwelling.

Another way to examine this problem is to look at the cost of consuming housing services. We have already assumed that all other costs are the same for these two families; the only cost of housing services that differs is the **implicit rental value** of each dwelling. The implicit rental value is what the family would have to pay to rent the same dwelling if it didn't own that dwelling. This is approximately equal to the opportunity cost of the total market value of each house per period. The statement by the family in the $500,000 house, "We could never afford to live in this house if we had to buy it," is wrong-headed. That family is already spending five times more each year for housing services than the family living in the otherwise identical dwelling that has a market value of $100,000.

When market housing values become high enough, families of modest means eventually react to the true opportunity cost of living in higher-priced houses. That's why we have seen at times families selling their homes for a hefty profit in cities in California and moving to less expensive cities in Oregon, Idaho, and Washington. Those families, at least in part, have decided that they were spending too much for housing services relative to their annual incomes.

The moral of this story is that when you own a home, you are paying for the opportunity cost of the current market value of that home—its implicit rental value—no matter what you paid for it originally or the size of your mortgage.

Interest Rates Are so High I Can't Afford to Buy a House, a Car, or a Big Boat

W hen you go to buy a house or a car or a boat, you will typically borrow a large part of the purchase price of that asset. When you go to borrow the money you will be faced with an array of interest rates that banks and other lending institutions will want to charge you. While there may be differences of a percentage point or so between loans that you can get, all of the interest rates may seem high to you. But in fact, depending on several factors, the interest rates charged to you on funds borrowed for a housing purchase, for example, may turn out to be relatively low, or even *negative*.

How can that be? you ask. How could I ever pay an interest rate that is negative? You will never actually pay a **market interest** rate that is negative. Market interest rates are always positive. But the **real, after-tax interest rate** that you end up paying may turn out to be below zero.

Consider an example. Suppose you buy a house and take out a mortgage on which the interest rate charged over a 30-year term is 8 percent. When you take out the mortgage, the rate of inflation has been 3 percent per year for the past decade. So your **expected real interest rate**, after you subtract the **expected rate of inflation**, is approximately 5 percent. Also, in most situations you are allowed to *deduct* mortgage interest payments from your taxable income before you pay federal income taxes. Let's say that you are in the 15 percent **tax bracket**. (See Chapter 5 in *Economics Today*.) On your 8 percent interest, 1.2 percent (8% x 15% = 1.2%) is thereby paid by Uncle Sam. That means that your real, after-tax, inflation-corrected, rate of interest that you are paying is (approximately) 8 percent minus 3 percent minus 1.2 percent, or 3.8 percent.

Let's say that 10 years later two things have happened. First, the rate of inflation in the economy has notched up to 8 percent and second, you got a much better, higher-paying job so that you are now in a higher tax bracket, paying a marginal tax rate of 36 percent. First of all, if you are paying a nominal rate of interest at 8 percent and inflation is 8 percent, your real rate of interest is 0 percent. Next you get a tax benefit of 36 percent of 8 percent, or 2.88 percent. In effect then your real, after-tax rate of interest that you are paying on your mortgage is a *minus* 2.88 percent.

What does all this mean? It means that you shouldn't look only at the market, or nominal, rate of interest charged on funds lent you. You should look at the current rate of inflation and what it has been in the past and come up with some estimate of what you think it will be in the future. Then you should also look at your marginal tax rate.[1] In so doing you can come up with the real after-tax rate of interest that you will be paying. It may be much less than you think it is.

Getting Tax Refunds

When you go to work, if you aren't working already, you will be asked to fill out a W-4 form. On this form you indicate the number of **tax exemptions** for which you qualify. If you have a family, you might put down three exemptions—you, your spouse, and your child. Your employer uses the number of exemptions so designated to determine (from a set of tax tables) how much she or he should deduct in **withholding taxes** every time you are paid. At the end of the year your employer gives you a W-2 form which shows you and the Internal Revenue Service (IRS) how much in taxes was deducted from your paychecks throughout the year.

Most people get all excited and think they are lucky when, after figuring out their taxes for the previous year, they determine that the IRS owes them a refund. In fact, a number of individuals fill out their W-4 forms in such a way as to increase

---

[1] You can only deduct the interest cost of a mortgage if you are *itemizing deductions* on your federal income tax return. For those individuals who do not, the marginal tax rate concept does not apply.

the size of the refund they get from the IRS each year. They do this by indicating *fewer* tax exemptions than they are allowed. In this way, their employer deducts more in withholding taxes than she or he would otherwise. The result is a larger total payment of taxes for the year and a greater chance of a refund the following year. In most circumstance (if not all), such action on your part will make you *worse* off, not better off.

In essence, what you are doing is giving the federal government an **interest-free loan** for the excess payments that you have made throughout the year. You are sacrificing the opportunity cost on all of the excess payments for the period from the time you make them to the time you get the refund. At a minimum, the opportunity cost is the after-tax rate of return that you could have earned had you put those excess payments in an interest-earning investment vehicle, such as **certificates of deposit (CDs)** or an interest-bearing account in a financial institution. You end up with a lower **net worth** and less spendable income when you get your tax refund than you would have if your employer had collected only the correct amount of taxes from each paycheck.

Consider an example. You are in the 28 percent marginal tax bracket. You claimed one less exemption than you should have. You end up getting a $600 refund. If you had put that cash in the bank at say an after-tax return of 5 percent interest per year, however, you would have earned $30 on top of the $600. You also would have had instant access to your cash, instead of having to wait for a refund.

Perhaps this is the only way you can force yourself to save, but if you have any will power at all, you will be better off using normal savings accounts for which you are paid a positive market interest rate.

Living Without Debt

How many times have you heard people say that they would be okay financially if they just didn't have so many bills to pay? I have heard such a statement on countless occasions throughout my life. Bills, bills, bills, they just seem to come all the time. Many people dream of a life without debt so that they would have no bills to pay. But does that really make sense? Probably not, at least for most people.

First of all, consider what a credit card or some type of **revolving credit account** really is. When you use the credit card, you do not immediately pay for your purchases. At the end of each month, you are given a choice—pay off all of the credit-card balance, or pay only part of it and pay interest on what remains. Certainly there is some reason to use credit cards even if you pay off all of the balance each month. In the first place, you do not have to carry around so much cash. So you remove some risk of theft of cash. Second, you have a record of your purchases. Third, it is often easier to get refunds for credit card purchases, particularly on purchases made through the mail.[2] But perhaps even more importantly, *you are able to get the use of the money you have spent via credit cards for part of the month before you pay your credit card balance.* In other words, because you don't have to pay off your credit-card account balance until the end of the month, you can have a higher bank balance during that time period. To the extent that you earn interest on that bank balance, you will be earning more interest by not paying off the credit-card account balance until the last day allowed before you are charged interest.

But there may be another reason to use credit cards or to go into debt in general. It has to do with what you are purchasing. Let's say that you have a goal in life to pay for things as you use them. When you buy a meal, that means that you pay cash for the meal. When you buy a ticket to a concert, you pay cash for that ticket. But what about when you buy a car or a house? You don't actually use up that car or house completely during the first month or even during the first year that you have it. What you do is obtain a **stream of services** throughout the asset's life or at least throughout your ownership of the asset. Therefore, even if you wanted to be conservative in your financial affairs and "pay as you go" (i.e., for everything as you use it), you would *want* to go into debt to pay for **long-lived assets**, such as cars and houses. You would want your debt repayment stream for those assets to match your **consumption stream** of those assets.

If you pay with cash for the full price of a car, so that you owe nothing, you are in effect **saving** much of the purchase price of the car. Saving is a provision for future consumption.

---

[2] Pursuant to the Fair Credit Billing Act of 1974.

Once you own the car you have a future stream of consumption available. As you use the car and it depreciates, you are in effect dissaving each year.

A typical example will demonstrate why the average person has to live in debt if he or she wants to purchase relatively expensive durable assets. Let's say that you earn $30,000 a year. You pay the following in taxes (approximately):

28%	to the federal government
7%	to the state government
7%	for Social Security (FICA)

If you add 8 percent that you pay into a company pension plan, that means approximately 50 percent of your income is left to spend each year. It would be pretty hard for you to buy a $15,000 car with cash and still have funds left over to pay for clothes, housing, and food. Typically, then, you will purchase the $15,000 car on time and make monthly payments to a bank or other financial institution that might give you credit.

Living in debt is reasonable for most people. Most people are better off by smoothing out their consumption purchases over a lifetime. They do this by going into debt on some occasions and saving on other occasions. There is no ultimate financial necessity, or advantage, to living with zero debt.

How Much Are You Willing to Pay for That New-Car Smell?

Many people know what it feels like to sit in a new car. Much of the feeling comes from the smell—the new-car smell—whether it comes from fine leather or less-expensive synthetic seat covers and carpets. For most people it's a good smell. They also like to know that no one else has done anything bad to the new car. It's like starting out with a clean slate. The important question, though, is how much are you really willing to pay for that new-car smell?

I am, of course, simplifying the issue. The purchase of a new car is more than just for the smell. In the decision to buy a new car versus a used car, you also know that with a new car you get a certain amount of increased warranty protection from the new-car dealer, and you don't have to worry about how the car was cared for previously. Additionally, you can make sure that all maintenance is carried out as it should be. Finally, you can order a new car with exactly the options you want.

In order to decide rationally whether you should pay for the benefits of a new rather than a used car, you have to know the marginal cost of the new-car purchase versus the used-car purchase. Otherwise stated, you have to know the true cost of, say, buying and owning a new car for one year.

The first cost you incur when you purchase a new car—or any asset for that matter—is the **cost of acquisition**. The cost of acquisition is defined as the difference between the purchase price of an asset and the *immediate* resale price. With respect to a new car, the cost of acquisition is rather dramatic. You may have to take a substantial loss of as high as 25 percent if you try to turn right around and resell your brand new car. The more unique the car, the higher is the cost of acquisition in percentage terms. For other assets, the cost of acquisition may be even higher than that of a new car. This is true for so-called high-end models of power boats, sailboats, and furniture.

Another important cost of owning a new car during its first year is the cost of depreciation. This can be measured by the difference between the *immediate* resale value of the car after its purchase (the purchase price minus its cost of acquisition) minus the resale value of the car at the *end of one year.* Depreciation occurs because of normal wear and tear on any machinery. Cars depreciate for another reason—they are considered relatively less desirable by car purchasers because newer cars embody improvements such as added safety features, different styling, and better audio systems. Relatively speaking, therefore, older cars, even in the absence of physical depreciation, are relatively less desirable than newer cars.

The cost of operation of the automobile for the first year typically would be a minor factor in making a decision between purchasing a new and a used car. After all, the cost of operation—gas, insurance, tune-ups, etc.—should be approximately the same for a new car as for one that is one year old.

The two most important costs associated with purchasing a new car relative to one that is a year old are the cost of acquisition and depreciation. For a $15,000 car, these two added together can be as high as $5,000. For a $25,000 car, they can be as high as $7,500. Is that new-car smell worth it? Only you can give the answer, but at least it will be based on an understanding of the true marginal cost of a one-year difference in the age of a car that you purchase.

So You've Just Won Your Lawsuit

Some of you at some time, somewhere, somehow will end up suing somebody else. And you might win. For example, you might get hurt in an automobile accident and sue the person at fault and his or her insurance company. Or a product may malfunction and injure you. The accident may reduce your ability to earn a living or you may be in a family in which the financial provider of the household is similarly injured.

In all of these cases, it is possible that the defendant, which is usually an insurance company acting on behalf of the person being sued, may try to settle with you prior to going to trial. Or if you go to trial and win, the defendant may offer you what is known as a **structured settlement**. If you win a lawsuit and get paid on the spot, that's called a **lump-sum payment**. With the structured settlement, in contrast, you are given a series of payments over time (which may or may not be equal in size) plus a large **balloon payment** at the end of the period, say 20 years from now. Alternatively, you may be offered large payments every five years.

Often the losing defendant's attorney will add up all of the proffered future payments and show you that you will be making more money this way. You might, for example, be given a choice between a lump-sum payment of $75,000, or a structured settlement of $10,000 for each year for 10 years. $10,000 multiplied by 10 equals $100,000, or one and a quarter times the lump-sum payment offered. Does that mean you are better off taking the lump-sum payment? The answer is, you don't know. You have to consider the **time value of money**. A dollar today does not have the same value as a promise to pay you a dollar next year, even if you are certain that you will get paid the dollar in one year. After all, there is an advantage to having the dollar today: you can place the dollar in a savings vehicle of some form and earn, say, 5 percent to 10 percent interest.

YEAR	DISCOUNT FACTOR 8%	PRESENT VALUE
1	.926	$9,260
2	.857	$8,570
3	.794	$7,940
4	.735	$7,350
5	.681	$6,810
6	.630	$6,300
7	.583	$5,830
8	.540	$5,400
9	.500	$5,000
10	.463	$4,630
TOTAL		**$67,090**

In Chapter 29 in *Economics Today* we refer to the calculation of today's valuation of any future income or cost as **discounting**. We look at the **present value** of money in the future. You have to do the same thing if you are ever offered any type of structured settlement. You have to discount the future promised payments back to today to determine the present value of the stream of payments. In the example above, we can calculate the present value of the offer from the insurance company. Let's use an interest rate (discount rate) of 8 percent.

At an 8 percent discount rate, the structured settlement offer is certainly not so good as the lump-sum payment offer. The lump-sum-payment deal is better. If the discount rate you use is higher than 8 percent, the present value of the structured settlement is even lower.

This same analysis can be applied to deciding whether you should purchase a lottery ticket.

Should I Purchase a Lottery Ticket?

A growing number of states have legal state-run lotteries, in which billions of dollars each year are bet. This dollar figure is increasing. References in everyday speech "If I win the lottery, I'll _____ [you fill in the blank]" are becoming part of our culture. In some states, TV shows have a nightly ritual in which the daily "lotto number" is chosen. In some cities there is a newspaper story once a week or so about someone who won $7, $8, $9, or $10 million or maybe even more. These numbers are false and misleading. Just as a structured settlement has to be discounted, so too does a payment of lottery winnings spread out in equal sums over 20 years.

Typical reported lottery winnings range from several million dollars to over $50 million. In some cases the payment stream is spread out over more than 20 years. When you consider the fact that the present value of a dollar received in 20 years at a 8 percent discount rate is only 21.5 cents, you can readily understand how lottery winnings are exaggerated.

This section is concerned with whether or not you should play the lottery. Even if the reported $20 million jackpots are worth much less when properly discounted, that's still more money than most of us will ever earn in a lifetime (or even two). But that doesn't necessarily mean the lottery is worth playing. To determine whether it's a "fair" game of chance you have to examine your chances (probability) of winning over some period of time and then multiply those chances times the possible winnings. You come up with an **expected value** of playing the lottery. Expected values are calculated by multiplying the probability of an event times the value of the outcome.

In order to make such calculations for the various state lotteries, you would have to find out how much is bet, how much is taken up by administrative costs from those bettings, how much is given to education and other designated sources, and how much is left over for the actual prizes and then how much you actually get in present value terms for those prizes.

The expected value of playing the lottery is low. My advice to you is to play the lottery only if you get consumption value approximately equal to the amount of money you are betting. If you are betting in the hopes that your net worth will change someday, you are right—you will become poorer than you would be otherwise because the expected value of playing the lottery is so close to zero compared to the non-zero cost of betting. That doesn't mean you should never bet, however. If you place an extremely high utility on the thought that you *might* win, then betting on the lottery might be okay. Gambling in any form is seldom an activity in which you as an individual player can expect in the long run to win. But gambling in and of itself generates utility for those who gamble. In that sense, gambling is no different than spending funds on a concert, a book, or a movie. It is the use of income today to yield consumption utility today.

Clearly, playing the lottery is not going to improve significantly your chances of having a better lifestyle in the future. But saving and placing what you save each year into some form of investment may improve your life later on. The question is, What investment?

There Must Be Some Way to Get Rich Quickly

I have already talked about investing in a house. As I indicated, there is no guarantee of an above-average rate of return for doing so. In Chapter 21 of *Economics Today* I point out that most, if not all, get-rich schemes should be shunned. Why? Think about it intuitively. We live in a competitive world. Almost everybody would like to make a higher-than-normal rate of return on his or her investments. If someone comes to you and offers you a get-rich scheme, you have to ask yourself why you are being offered this great benefit—the ability to make a higher-than-normal rate of return. The answer is typically that you are being offered that ability only if you are willing to take a higher-than-normal **risk**. Remember always:

> **There is a positive correlation between risk and rate of return.**

In a competitive world, higher rates of return are associated with higher degrees of risk. There is really no way out of this **"iron law of investing"** as long as we live in a world of scarce resources in which people are competing in order to better themselves.

I am sure you have seen some of the ads by self-professed, self-made multi-millionaires who offer, for a mere $19.95, to let you in on their secrets of instant success. Some of these ads may tell you that "You, too, can earn $60,000 a month without risking anything" or, "You, too, can learn to buy land with no money down and make yourself rich."

An advertisement that I see often has the following headline: "You can make up to $9800 in 24-hours!" A personalized letter follows:

Dear Friend,
I made $9,800 in 24 hours. You may do better! I own four homes in Southern California. The one I am living in now in Beverly Hills is worth more than $1 million.

My suggestion to you is to read such ads and laugh. I am not saying that the authors of those ads didn't make a lot of money income. They may have even made it doing the very thing they want to teach you. But the fact that you and thousands of others can find out this valuable information on "how to get rich quickly," either for free or for some small payment for a book, cassette, or lecture series, guarantees that whatever valuable information the author originally had has already become public information. **Public information** has *zero* value in allowing you to make a higher-than-normal rate of return.

I know that throughout your life you will have well-meaning friends and relatives who will want to give you hot tips about stocks to buy, or companies to invest in, or businesses to start. You will be presented with schemes that surely can't fail and with investments that are too good to be true. My advice is that you step back and remember this basic course in economics in which you were taught that all the players in our economy are competing for scarce resources. The old saying, you get what you pay for, really has an economic basis. In a competitive world, if someone offers you free advice about how to get rich, that advice is worth just what you paid!

Always ask yourself the following question: If the deal is so good, why is the person telling me about it? Or you might ask yourself, "If the information is so valuable, why doesn't this person who is giving it to me simply use it, become a multi-billionaire, and not bother with people like me?" I have often wondered why stockbrokers, for example, can be so certain about the hot tips that they give their clients. If they are so certain, why are they still stockbrokers, instead of just super-rich investors?

Well, you may be saying to yourself right now, where does that leave me? How should I invest my hard-earned savings? There is no specific answer, but rather a general operating rule:

Diversify your assets

Diversification is the cornerstone to rational investing. Diversification simply means that you don't put too much of your total wealth into any one asset. That means that you don't have all of your net worth tied up in real estate, or in the stock market, or in the bond market, or in rare coins, or in antiques, or in fine art. Diversification means that you take a balanced approach to investing and make sure you have some of each of many assets.

Using Economics to Filter the News

For the rest of your life, you are going to be bombarded with news. You'll read it in the newspaper, hear it on the radio, see it on TV. For the rest of your life, you are going to read or listen to political speeches. Basic economics can help you distinguish real news from political pap. There are two starting points that you have to remember all of the time:

1. Bad news sells.
2. Worse news sells even better.

What you read, hear about, and see on the news is a result of people in the news media competing for your eyes, ears, and dollars. The result is a focus on bad news, and an attempt to exaggerate every negative aspect of anything that ever happens. The outcome is that what you are seeing, hearing, and reading is not necessarily representative of what is actually happening in the world on any given day. Rather it generally represents the bad part of what is happening in the world.

From the above discussion it follows that you should:

Always be skeptical of any *reported* crisis.

The news media are always looking for a new crisis. Nothing sells news more than a crisis. In my lifetime I have lived through a meat crisis, a food crisis, an energy crisis, a new ice-age crisis, a global-warming crisis, an educational crisis, an inflationary crisis, a disinflationary crisis, an interest-rate crisis, a smog crisis, and a nutritional crisis. I am sure there have been others, but this list is long enough. I am not saying that the problems just mentioned did not exist, but it's not clear how many of them were really crises.

To make a crisis situation even worse, journalist like to tack on dire-sounding adjectives. So:

**You should especially beware of any-
thing called a *permanent* crisis.**

I remember back when news articles told me that we were going to have a permanent food crisis. I remember during different years when I was told that we were in for a permanent energy crisis.

Well, the supply of food didn't dry up, nor did the supply of energy. Remarkably, not only did the permanent food crisis disappear, so did the permanent energy crisis. The relative price of food did not go to the moon, nor did the price of energy. In **nominal terms**, for example, a gallon of gas is certainly more today than it was in the early 1950's. In **real terms**—corrected for inflation—the price of a gallon of gas today is *less* than it was in 1950. One thing that journalists and politicians never seem to understand for very long is that people react to changing **relative prices**. When the relative price of gas went up in the 1970s, two things occurred: (1) consumers cut back on their consumption, and (2) suppliers looked for more oil. Lo' and behold, suppliers found more oil. They also developed better techniques for getting the oil out of the ground. Hence the real price of oil products fell.

Indeed, you should be suspicious of any article that tells you that we're in for a permanent crisis if that means that we're going to run out of some scarce commodity. Well before we run out of anything in this world, the relative price will have risen so high that we won't be using it anymore. Rather, we will use substitutes.

In the political arena, you have to be aware that opportunity cost is lurking around every corner of every hallway in

Congress. Every time a politician tells you that we have a crisis and therefore we have to spend government revenues to solve it, that means that (1) we won't spend funds on something else or (2) a larger fraction of total annual output—GDP—will be going toward government expenditures. That doesn't mean that we shouldn't spend the funds or have the program; all it means is that "there ain't no such thing as a free lunch." Every action by every political entity has an opportunity cost. It is virtually impossible to have more of everything at the same time. We can have more of everything over time through **economic growth**, but never at the same time. That's what the **production possibilities curve** shows in Chapter 2. I don't propose that you draw one of these for your local member of Congress, but at least you should be aware of the necessary trade-offs that occur anytime a government undertakes to solve a problem by spending more government revenues (taxes).

Career Choices

An important factor in determining what type of lifestyle you are going to have is making the right choice for your career. In this discussion I assume that most of you have not yet chosen a career. Some of you are in a business school and know you want to get a degree in business—either a B.A. or an M.B.A. Many of you, however, are simply taking economics in order to satisfy a social sciences requirement.[3] A rational career choice requires at a minimum the following:

1. A knowledge of yourself, including your skills, abilities, likes, dislikes, strong points, weak points.
2. A knowledge of available careers, including their education and training requirements, as well as their potential salaries.
3. A strong dose of realism.

---

[3] Some of you may be doing what I did as an undergraduate. I chose economics as a major because it required the fewest credits, thereby leaving me more time to take other courses. Why I ended up being an economist anyway is another story.

ON BEING REALISTIC

L et's take this third point first because it seems so out of place. What I mean by a strong dose of realism is the understanding that for most of us there is no easy way to settle into a career that within a relatively short period of time will yield complete job satisfaction, a pleasant working environment, congenial colleagues, six-weeks' vacation per year with full pay, a company-provided Mercedes-Benz, a terrific pension, and a salary in six figures. Let's look at the reality of income figures in the United States. In 1998 the **median income** for a family of four was estimated to be around $45,000. That's **gross income**. Remember we're taking about a family of four. You may be thinking that that is not even enough money income to live well as a single person. What would you think is a good salary even for the head of a family of four? Okay, so you picked $70,000. Do you know that if you made $70,000 you'd be in the top 10 percent of income earners in the United States? What about $100,000. Then you'd move into the top 4 percent of income earners.

The point I am trying to make is a simple one: you can't really expect to be paid more than your **marginal revenue product**, which you will read about in Chapter 27. What determines your value to any employer? What you can produce and what that product can be sold for. You have relatively little say over what your product can be sold for, but you can determine what you can produce. You determine this by developing your skills and abilities; this is done through training and schooling. What does that mean? Simply that you have to seek training, whether it be in school or on the job, and you can't expect to be rewarded more than you are worth to an employer.

I am not saying that you should "get all the education you can get." I dispelled that notion early on in this booklet. But realize that the more you do to make yourself potentially productive to an employer, the higher you can expect your income to be, at least eventually. It's not surprising that general-purpose humanities' degree holders earn less than specifically trained computer scientists, for example, even when both groups have exactly the same number of years of schooling. This does not mean a humanities' education is worthless and that everyone should become computer scientist. Rather, this is the dose of reality that I referred to earlier. If you spend your life doing things that are fun and enjoyable for you, you normally cannot necessarily expect the market to reward you. You'll have to get your reward from the satisfaction you receive from doing something you like—it won't usually come in the form of a higher paycheck.

In the job market, the more desirable the job, the more fun it is to do, the more glamorous it is, the more it involves exotic travel, the more "perks" it seems to have, then the more competition there will be for that job, and therefore the lower the entry-level salary. It's not surprising that people who want to break into the movie business, the video business, the music business, and the art business must expect to earn virtually nothing in the beginning and must expect to work extremely hard. Is this unfair? Economics is silent about the issue of fairness for that involves normative analysis. Positive economic analysis simply provides the dose of reality.

KNOW THYSELF

Career planning involves knowing thyself—obtained through self assessment. That is something you can do in the hands of a competent career guidance counselor. Most colleges and universities offer this service free of charge. If it is not available, somebody, somewhere on your campus will be able to steer you to a guidance counselor who can give you a battery of tests so that you might find out things about yourself that can help you decide what to do.[4]

FINDING OUT ABOUT CAREERS

Career information is plentiful. The federal government puts out numerous publications. All are available in the reference section of your library. The most important are the following:

---

[4] Permit me another personal footnote here. I took all those tests as a senior in high school and was told that I should become a technician. My counselor warned me against a career that required written English. (Do not believe everything you are told.)

1. *Occupational Outlook Handbook (OOH).* This is the best source of general information about occupations, about 250 of which are described in detail. These occupations account for about 80 percent of all jobs. Each occupation description tells about the nature of work and the working conditions as well as training, required qualifications, and possibilities for advancement. Also go to O*NET on the World Wide Web.
2. *Dictionary of Occupational Titles (DOT).* In this publication, over 20,000 different kinds of jobs are listed and given a specific number. Perusal of the *DOT* reveals jobs that most people don't even know exist.
3. *Guide for Occupational Exploration (GOE).* This publication divides careers into groups according to interest. There are twelve groups called interest areas. The *GOE* gives a definition of each interest area and then explains it in more detail. If you know what your strongest interests are, the *GOE* can be extremely helpful.

Careers in Economics

I am an economist and you are taking an economics course so I think you need to know about what awaits you if you choose a career in economics. I am not going to argue for or against such a career.[5] What I do want to do is present some information about what economists do and how you might go about becoming one.

TRAINING IN ECONOMICS

After you finish this basic undergraduate course in principles of economics, if you decide to major in economics you'll go on to take more advanced courses in micro- and macroeconomics theory. You might take courses in the applied areas of microeconomics such as industrial organization and labor economics. The applied courses in macroeconomics

---

[5] Looking backwards, it is said that hindsight gives you 20-20 vision (and choosing economics was the best career choice I could have made).

will almost always include money and banking. You might specialize in an area such as international economics, environmental economics, economic development, or public finance.

If you choose to continue your education after your undergraduate work in economics, you can obtain a master's degree or a Ph.D. in economics. Alternatively, you can go into a business school program and obtain a master's in business administration (MBA) at one of the graduate schools of business. An MBA prepares you for a career in business management. Much of the content of an MBA program is based on economics because economics provides the theoretical background for business courses.

Besides being excellent preparation for an MBA, an economics undergraduate major provides a good preparation for those of you who wish to attend law school. Potential lawyers will want to have training in economics, accounting, and the presentation of ideas in written form in particular.

Economics as an undergraduate major also provides training for those of you who wish to go to graduate school in public administration or public policy. Master's degrees in those areas allow you to more easily enter a career in government service.

WHAT ECONOMISTS DO

Economists work for colleges and universities, government agencies, and business firms. Economists study how scarce resources are allocated. Such a study may involve forecasting how good overall national economic activity will be next year. This is called **business forecasting**. For a particular business firm, an economist may analyze how many additional warehouses a large clothing chain might wish to maintain. Economists often work for attorneys in estimating lost earnings capacity in cases involving death or injury, or estimating the value of assets in messy divorce trials.

Most economists work for businesses. Of the approximately 65,000 individuals who classify themselves as economists, almost half work for business firms. About 25,000 work as teachers or researchers, mainly in colleges and universities. The remainder are employed by government at the local, state, and federal levels.

Why Economics is Good Training No Matter What You Do

You may decide that economics would be a good major for you in college. You may even decide that it would become a good career. But there are other reasons for wanting to study economics. In short, the training you will receive as an undergraduate major in economics does the following:

By learning economics, you learn how to think in a way that is applicable to just about everything that you see, do, or read.

Economics deals with vital current problems at the national level such as inflation, unemployment, pollution, poverty, health care, and economic growth. Economics is a *problem-based* social science. The problems with which it is concerned are the central issues of our times, the ones you read about in newspapers and magazines and hear about on radio and television. They pervade all of politics.

And as you have seen in this short guide, economic analysis can be applied to your everyday life. Economics at its heart is a very practical social science.

Use it.